Visions and Inspirations

Edwin H Rydberg

This is a project borne from the melding of often ancient human wisdom with fledgling machine intelligence. I hope you agree that the result can be beautiful and inspiring.

Most of the quotes are of human origin, although a few were generated by machine. If no attribution is given, the quote has either an anonymous source or has been generated by Chat-GPT3 (already an antiquated old-timer, less than two years after its birth to the world). Images were created by Midjourney using my own prompts. The front cover image was generated by DALL-E.

- edwin h rydberg

This book is copyright © 2025 Edwin H Rydberg.

Published by Quantum Dot Press

The SKY isn't the limit – the SKY has no limit.

Sarah Barker

> The fishermen know that the sea is dangerous and the storm terrible, but they have never found these dangers sufficient reason for remaining ashore.
> — Vincent van Gogh

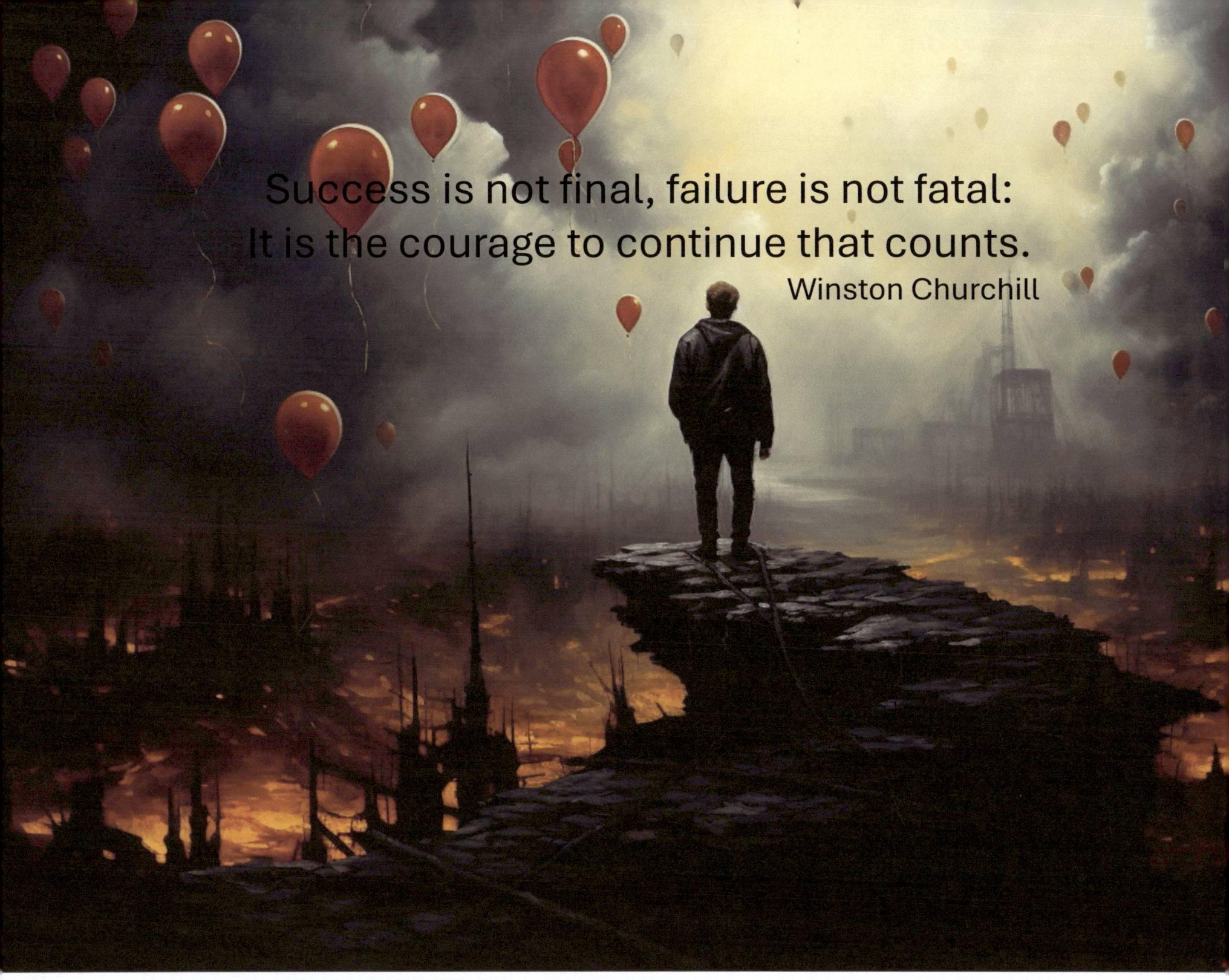

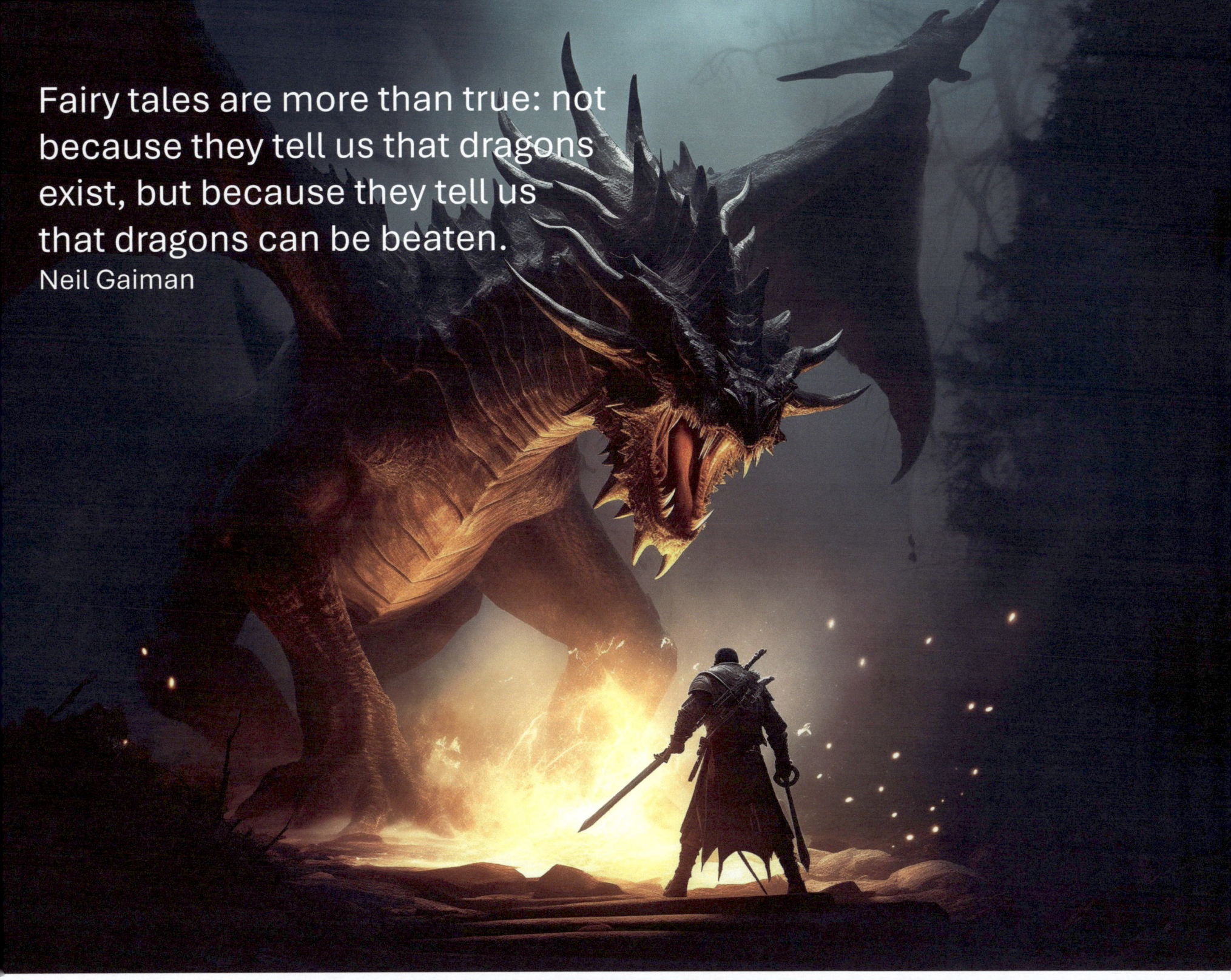

Live as if you were to die tomorrow.
Learn as if you were to live forever.
   Mahatma Ghandi

> The first step towards getting somewhere, is to decide you're not going to stay where you are.
>
> JP Morgan

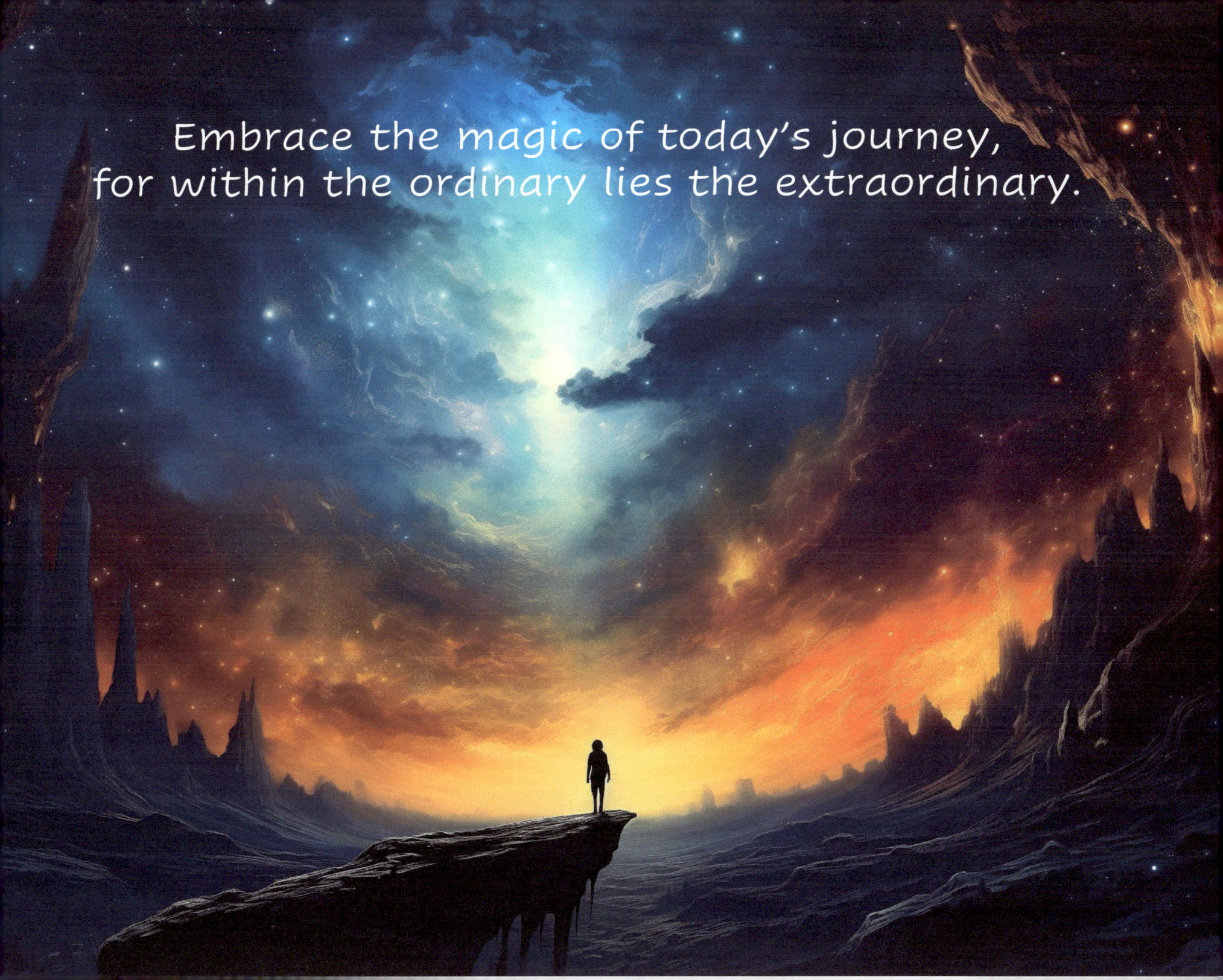

Don't worry about the world coming to an end today.
It's already tomorrow in Australia.
Charles Schultz

Do what you feel in your heart to be right – for you'll be criticized anyway.
Eleanor Roosevelt

Don't limit your challenges.
Challenge your limits.
Anonymous

Embrace the winds of transformation, for they have the power to shape us into resilient beings, capable of reaching heights we never thought possible.

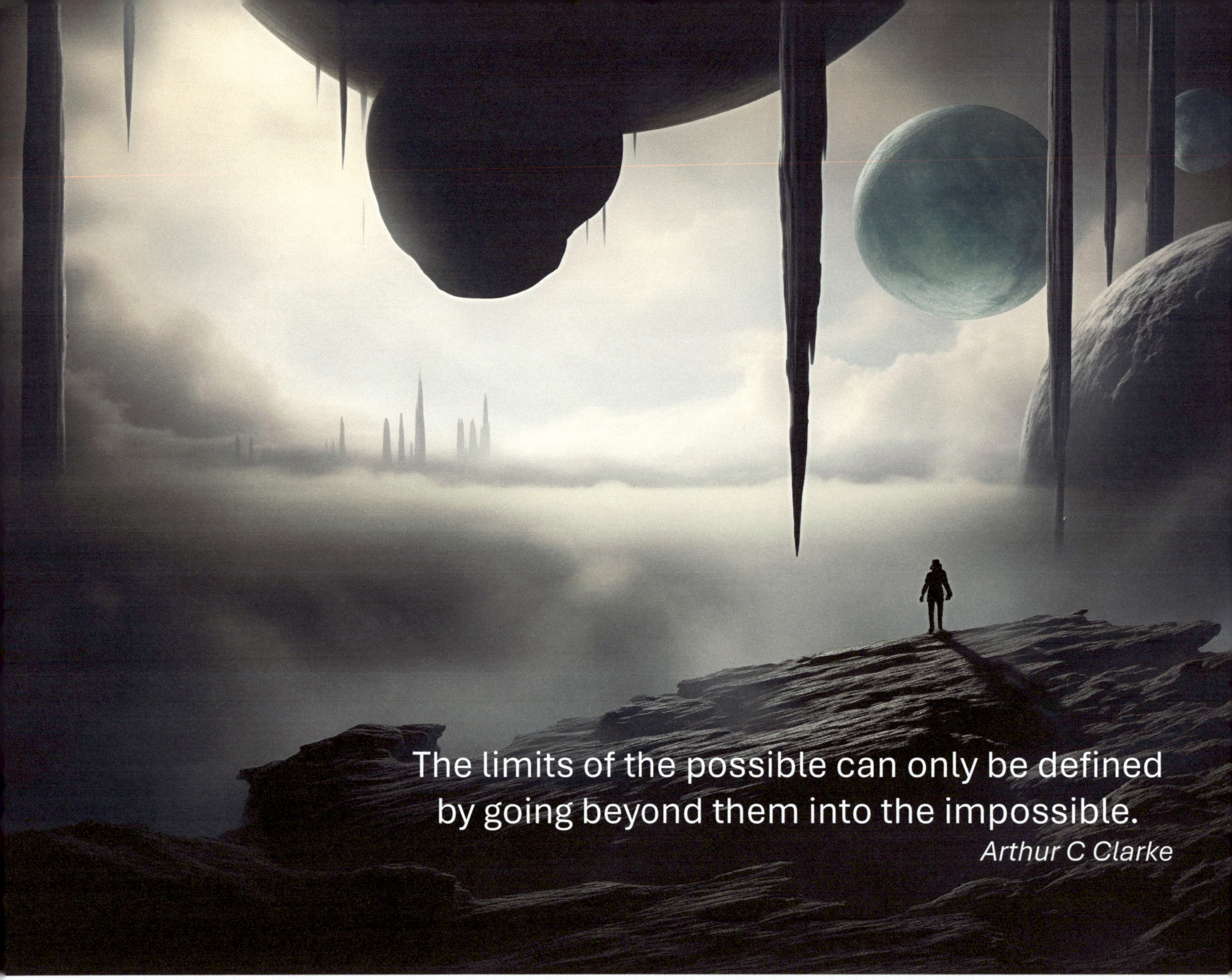

I'm not going to continue knocking that old door that doesn't open for me.

I'm going to create my own door and walk through that.
Ava DuVerney

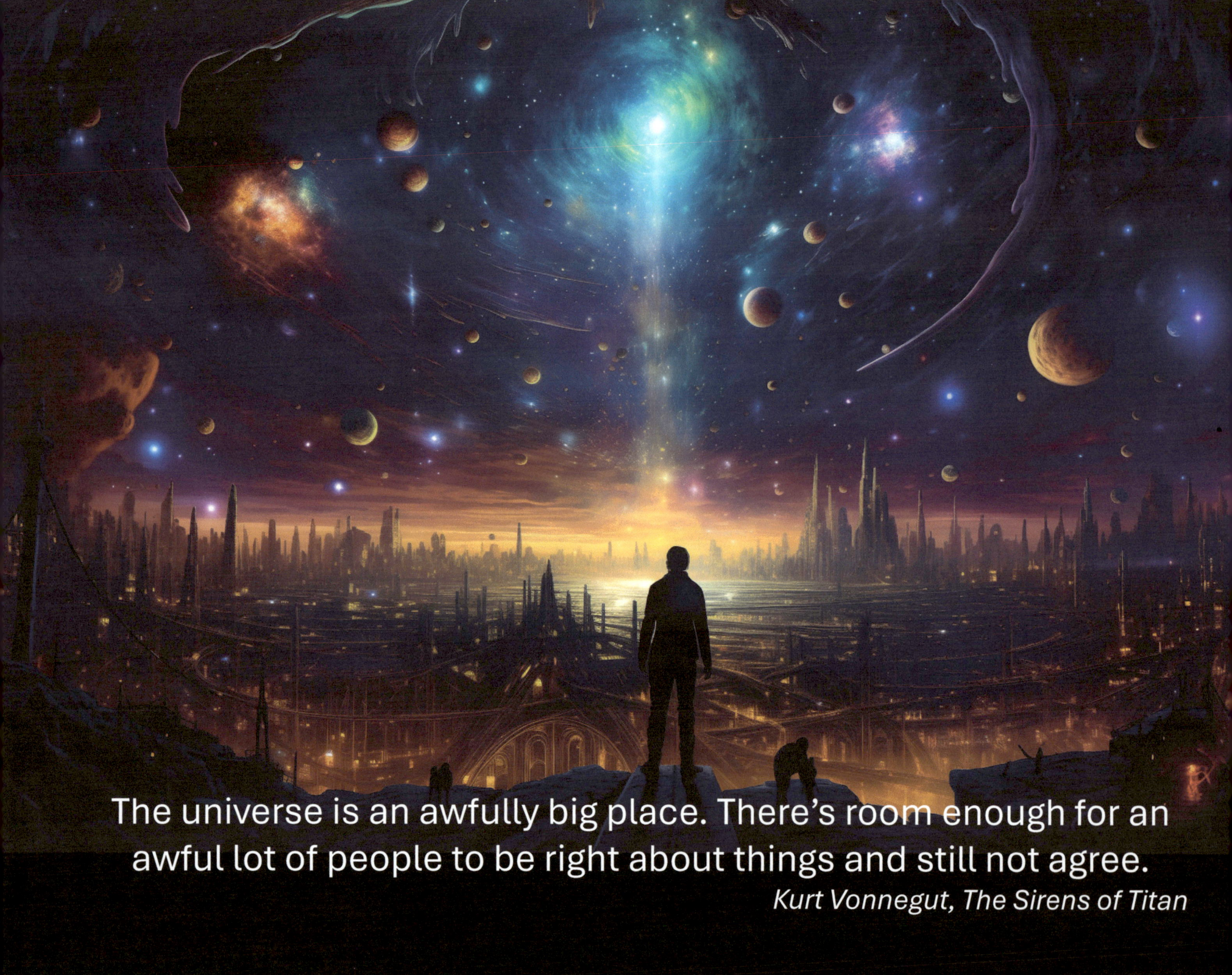

About Edwin H Rydberg

Author, publisher, and podcaster, Edwin H Rydberg has the unusual and somewhat contradictory characteristic of being a dreamer shackled with the character of a realist.

This may come as a result of spending the first half of life interrogating the workings of nature, and the second half questioning the meaning of existence.

You can find links to Edwin H Rydberg's various endeavours online at:

linktr.ee/ehrydberg

Now go out into the world and "fight, win, and call when you get back, darling, I enjoy your visits." – Edna Mode (The Incredibles)

Someday we'll find it,
    The Rainbow Connection.

The Lovers,
    The Dreamers,
and Me.

– Paul Williams and Kenneth Ascher